Responsible Pet Care

Turtles

Responsible Pet Care

Turtles

CARLIENNE FRISCH

Rourke Publications, Inc.
Vero Beach, FL 32964

Library of Congress Cataloging-in-Publication Data

Frisch, Carlienne, 1944–
     Turtles / by Carlienne A. Frisch
        p. cm. – (Responsible pet care)
     Summary: Information on choosing a turtle for a pet with instructions for caring for and feeding it.
        ISBN 0-86625-194-4
        1. Turtles as pets–Juvenile literature. [Turtles as pets.] I. Title.
     II. Series: Responsible pet care (Vero Beach, Fla.)
     SF459.T8F75 1991
     639.3'92-dc20   90-44221
                                                              CIP
                                                               AC

CONTENTS

Why Choose A Turtle?

A pet turtle isn't warm and furry, like a dog or a cat. It won't come when its name is called, but a turtle is an easy-going pet. It can be handled to make it tame, and it can learn to eat from your hand.

A North American Indian legend goes that all animals on earth once lived on the back of a giant turtle. The Native Americans believed that this turtle was very wise and friendly. They also believed that turtles gave good advice—if only people would listen!

Turtles have been around for two million years. They are related to the huge dinosaurs that once lived on the earth. Turtles are reptiles, which means they are **cold-blooded**. Their body temperature is about the same as that of the air or water around them. Their relatives include snakes, lizards, alligators, and crocodiles. Turtles are unique—they are the only reptiles with a shell. When a turtle senses danger, it pulls its head and legs under its tough shell.

This three-striped mud turtle is an aquatic turtle. Its webbed feet help it swim.

The red-eared slider is
one of the easiest turtles
to maintain.

There are more than 200 kinds of turtles in the world.
Those that live in water are called aquatic turtles. They
usually have flattened feet with webbed toes, which
help them swim. Land turtles, which live only on the
land, are sometimes called tortoises. Their feet are
usually shaped a bit like a club. The terrapin was
named by the Native Americans. This kind of turtle
lives both on land and in the water. Aquatic turtles,
tortoises, and terrapins may all be called turtles.

Turtles are easy to feed, and they are not hard to care
for if you learn how to do it. They live for a long time,
have good eyesight, and a keen sense of smell. Loud
noises don't bother them. They make good pets for
people unable to have a dog or a cat in their home.

Varieties of Turtles

Turtles from countries in Europe and Asia should not be adopted as pets. Some **species** are dying out in nature and should never be taken from their areas. Others need much extra care to keep them healthy. Most do not remain healthy during their trip to America.

Most experts agree that one common turtle makes a poor pet—the snapping turtle. This turtle lives in eastern North America. It has a mean personality and will eat almost anything. It has even bitten off people's toes and fingers!

There are many turtles from North America that do make good pets, however. The spotted turtle and musk turtle are found from Canada to Florida. The spotted turtle has orange spots on its shell. The musk turtle has pieces of flesh on its head, called **barbels**, that look like worms. When an animal comes close to eat the "worms," the musk turtle eats it instead!

The alligator snapping turtle lives along the Mississippi River. It has a spiny shell—and a mean bite!

The four-eyed turtle comes from Asia. It gets its name from the eye-like markings on the top of its head.

The painted turtle lives throughout the United States. It has a colorful shell that looks like it was painted. As the turtle gets older, the colors fade. The mud turtle lives along the Mississippi River and the rivers that run into it.

The gopher tortoise is the only true North American tortoise. It lives in the deserts of the southern United States and Mexico. It sleeps during the day and looks for food at night, when it is cooler.

The turtle that is easiest to care for is the red-eared turtle. It is the turtle most often found in pet stores. A young red-eared turtle is about the size of a half-dollar. It grows to be about 10 inches across. It is brightly colored and has a red patch or stripe near its ears. In nature, it lives in the central United States in slow-moving water. It likes to come out and sun itself on the shore.

Some varieties of turtles eat plants, some eat meat, and some eat both. Plant-eating turtles are probably the easiest to maintain.

Understanding Your Turtle

Turtles cannot whine or cry when they are uncomfortable or hungry. Their faces do not show if they are happy or sad. Therefore, a turtle's owner must learn to take care of a turtle to keep it healthy and safe.

A turtle withdraws into its shell when it feels threatened. It is important not to pick up the turtle when it is inside its shell. In the wild, only an enemy picks up a withdrawn turtle—so the turtle feels even more danger. Turtles should not be put on their backs, either. Sometimes they cannot turn themselves over and they will die.

The shell consists of two parts, usually joined by bony bridges. The top part is a **carapace**, which means "shield" in Spanish. The bottom is the **plastron**, which means "breastplate" in Italian. Both parts are made of bony plates or shields covered with **lamina**. Lamina is hard, like a fingernail. This coating gives the turtle its color.

A turtle withdraws into its shell when it feels threatened.

The bottom part of a turtle's shell is called the plastron. Note the clawed, stubby feet of this red-footed tortoise.

The shell is a live organ, like a heart or a stomach. It can pick up very small vibrations from the ground. In nature, these mean danger to the turtle. So, the owner must try to avoid vibrations. The terrarium, which is the turtle's house, should rest on rubber or felt cushions.

A turtle cannot hear voices. Instead, it "feels" low-pitched sounds, such as footsteps or tapping on the terrarium. A turtle has good eyesight and an excellent sense of smell. Because strange sights and odors make a turtle nervous, the terrarium should be placed where the turtle will not see a lot of activity. It also is a good idea to avoid strong smells, such as tobacco smoke.

When the turtle lies flat in natural or artificial lights, with legs and head stretched out, it is taking a sunbath. In autumn, if it becomes less active and doesn't want to eat, don't worry—it is getting ready to **hibernate**. If, however, a turtle swims restlessly, or digs holes, there may be something wrong with the climate in the terrarium. If two turtles ram their shells together, or bite each other, they may be getting ready to mate.

Buying A Turtle

A turtle can be bought from a pet store or from someone who puts an ad in the newspaper. It's fairly common for people to sell a turtle before they take a long vacation. They may also want to sell their terrarium and equipment. A few people will give away their turtle to a good home.

You should watch your turtle carefully before buying. Ask the owner if it is active during the day or in the evening. Find out when the turtle eats, and pay a visit during feeding time. If you don't see it eating after a couple of days, you should not buy the turtle. A healthy turtle will be hungry at least every other day, and it will eagerly hold onto your fingers with its front legs.

Turtles come in all shapes and sizes. The elongate tortoise has a long, rather narrow body and shell.

The box turtle is shaped almost like a square, with bright markings on its plastron.

You will want to find out how old your turtle is and how long it is expected to live. Some turtles live to be 80 years old. If you get a young turtle, find out how large it will become. Within two or three years, most baby turtles will grow to four times their size. You also will want to know if your turtle hibernates in winter. This information will help avoid surprises.

Even experts cannot tell if a young turtle is a male or a female. So, it is difficult to get a young turtle of a specific sex. But don't worry—either sex makes a good pet.

A dealer who sells turtles should provide the full scientific name of the turtle on the bill. The scientific name for the red-eared turtle, for example, is *Chrysemys scripta elegans*. There are two other turtles that look like the red-eared turtle. They have different scientific names.

The scientific name informs the owner that the turtle isn't an **endangered species** being sold under another name. It also will come in handy when the owner needs special advice if the turtle starts behaving strangely.

13

The Terrarium

A regular turtle tank or aquarium makes a good terrarium for a turtle. A ready-made terrarium of the right size can be bought, unless your turtle is quite large. The owner of an aquarium shop can tell you the proper size and how to set up the terrarium.

One or two baby turtles, about two inches across, may be kept in an aquarium that holds 8–10 gallons of water. It should have a cover, a heater, a thermometer to check temperature, and (for water turtles) a piece of cork bark to serve as an island. You will also need an adjustable desk lamp of about 60 watts. The lamp should shine on the cork island from about one foot away during daylight hours. When the turtles have grown to five or six inches across, they will need a bigger home.

Shells, branches, and plants provide the land turtle with an interesting environment. The water dish lets the turtle drink and swim.

The pancake tortoise is round and flat. Unlike other turtles, its shell is quite soft, allowing it to squeeze into tight places.

A water turtle needs an area five times as long and three times as wide as the length of its shell. The water in the aquarium should be about a foot deep.

A land turtle, even a baby, needs an area in length and width that is five times the length of its shell. A land turtle with a five-inch shell needs a space of 25 x 25 inches. A deep bowl or pan set into one corner of the terrarium lets the turtle swim and drink. It is easy to remove and clean the bowl and to change the water. There should be stone steps going into the basin. The turtle needs to be able to rest while partly in the water.

For either land or water turtles, the bottom of the terrarium should be covered with four inches of sand or gravel. For land turtles, add several inches of clean soil. You may then plant moss, small ferns, and other plants. Rocks and stones can be put in as hills and resting places.

The terrarium should be kept at about 80 degrees F. It should never drop below 68 degrees.

The First Few Days

A turtle purchased from a pet store may need a bath when it reaches its new home. A bowl of lukewarm water with one tablespoon of salt per quart of water is good. Let the turtle drink if it wants to. The salt helps the turtle if it has had diarrhea. The turtle should be cleaned gently and rinsed in fresh water.

The shell and skin should be checked for injuries or parasites, such as ticks or mites. If the turtle looks healthy, you can put it in the terrarium. At first, it will probably hide. This is perfectly normal. Let the turtle come out on its own. You should offer fresh food every day. A plant-eating turtle should be hungry after one or two days. A meat or fish eater will eat in five days or less. It is a good idea to take a sample of the first **feces** and have a veterinarian check it for parasites.

Before buying a turtle, the buyer should carefully examine the skin and shell for wounds or parasites.

Small turtles, like this four-month-old painted turtle, do not need a large terrarium to be happy.

Your turtle will choose a sleeping area, a digging area, and a place it considers a "toilet." If the toilet area is outside of the water, it will be easy for you to remove the feces and some of the surrounding soil.

The turtle should be fed in a cool, dry spot—not under the lamp. Offer fresh food daily. Turtles enjoy variety, and you can occasionally feed your turtle hay instead of fresh, juicy food. You can also let the turtle think it's raining by using lukewarm water in a spray bottle.

Turtles do not eat well under stress. Other pets, such as dogs, cats, or guinea pigs, must not go near the turtle. If they bite it, even in fun, the turtle could die. Inadequate terrarium space, strong vibrations, too much excitement around the terrarium, or being picked up when withdrawn into the shell all cause a turtle stress. Stress is a major cause of sickness. A sick turtle needs to be taken to a veterinarian.

Care And Maintenance

It is important to keep the terrarium clean. For a land turtle, the water in the basin should be changed daily. Feces, flaked-off skin, and leftover food have to be removed every day. The entire aquarium should be cleaned every three to six months. If the turtle has no worms and creates a toilet in only one or two places, the sand and soil need to be changed twice a year. Otherwise, a change is necessary every three months.

The water turtle's water should be changed every one to three days, depending on various conditions. If a water filter is used, the water should be changed three times a week. One change a week is enough if there are at least 25 gallons of water per pound of turtle. It is all right to use tap water that has reached room temperature.

The three-toed box turtle is found mainly in the southeastern United States.

A turtle's claws must be trimmed regularly.

Turtles need the claws on their feet trimmed. A nail clipper can be used, but whatever you use, be careful! If cut too far back, the claw will bleed. A turtle that spends time digging or walking on dry ground wears down its claws, so they can be trimmed less often.

The turtle's beak may also need trimming. If the turtle eats harder foods, such as small seeds, cuttlebone, and fibrous vegetable stems, the beak is worn down naturally. If not, the beak's horny edges should be filed down. A veterinarian can show you how to trim the claws and beak.

A land turtle that is kept in a very dry atmosphere may get cracks in its shell. A tiny bit of white petroleum jelly rubbed into the shell every two or three months will help keep the top layers more elastic.

In caring for your turtle, you must also consider your own health. Turtles can give people intestinal bacteria that cause diarrhea and stomach cramps. Though not usually serious, these problems can be avoided. Wash your hands with soap and water after handling your turtle or cleaning its equipment.

Feeding Your Turtle

Turtles need a wide choice of food. Feed a plant-eating turtle blossoms, wildflower seeds, berries, fruits, tomatoes, lettuce, and vegetables of the cabbage family. You must make sure not to give the turtle poisonous plants.

A turtle that also eats meat can have snails, insects, worms, or beetles that have just been killed. Besides these foods, a turtle that eats only meat can also be given fish or hamburger. It will not need vegetables, fruits, or other plants.

Turtles that eat only plants are called vegetarian. If they eat plants and animals, they are omnivorous. These two kinds of turtles should be fed five or six times a week. They can be fed twice a day during the times they seem most active. Turtles that eat only meat are carnivorous. They should be fed twice a week.

These African spur-thighed tortoises are making a meal out of raw sweet potatoes.

Most pet stores carry a variety of foods made especially for turtles.

If two turtles of different sizes are kept together, the larger one could bite off the smaller one's head if both try to eat the same food at the same time. It is important to feed them in separate parts of the terrarium. Land turtles should get food on a shallow dish on land. Place food for water turtles in the water.

You may want to chop the food to bite-size pieces for water turtles. A land turtle, however, will tear the food apart with its claws. If the turtle has a favorite food, it should not get it at every feeding. This will force the turtle to eat a varied diet. It needs all kinds of food for good nutrition.

The turtle also needs vitamins and minerals. Dry cat food is a good source of these. Some turtle owners also drop a lump of plaster of Paris into the water to provide calcium.

Leftover food, especially if it is in the water, should be removed as soon as the turtle leaves the feeding area. The food dish needs to be washed. To avoid shocking the turtle, allow fresh water to reach room temperature before being added to the land turtle's bowl or pan.

Wintering Over

Turtles that are natives of areas where winters are cold become less active in October. They are getting ready to hibernate. If they stop eating for several days in a row, it is time for the owner to stop feeding the turtle. It should be bathed daily for at least 10 minutes in water of 75–80 degrees F. to help clean out the intestines. It is also wise to have the feces checked so any problem can be treated before hibernation.

A water turtle can be left at the bottom of the terrarium without food. The water, however, needs to be cooled down over two or three weeks. It should be 40–47 degrees F. The water turtle will rest in it for one to two months. The water will not need changing.

You must prepare more for a land turtle's hibernation. After the turtle has been bathed, the terrarium temperature should be allowed to drop to about 68 degrees. When the turtle's activity slows down, it is time to move it to its winter home where a temperature of 42–45 degrees F. can be maintained. A cellar is the best place.

The three-striped mud turtle is a water turtle. During hibernation, it can be left at the bottom of the terrarium without food.

The leopard tortoise gets its name from its spotted shell.

A grown land turtle needs a box no smaller than 28 x 28 x 28 inches. It should have one-eighth-inch spaces between its boards so air can enter. Cover the bottom of the box with four inches of damp (not wet) lava clinker or fired clay beads. Then fill the box about three-fourths full with dry peat moss, dry leaves, or wood chips. Most of these items can be bought at a gardening supply store. A wire screen cover must be put on to keep the turtle from falling out of its box in case it walks in its sleep! Check every two weeks to make sure the turtle is safe.

When the turtle wakes up, put it back into the terrarium. After a few days, bring the temperature up to 80 degrees F. Before the turtle is fed the first time, it must be given a bath. It needs moisture before food. Some turtles won't eat for a few days; others will wait a couple of weeks.

Young, small turtles should not be allowed to hibernate. They do not have enough food in them to be able to skip eating during hibernation. Some fully-grown turtles never hibernate.

23

Health And Ailments

There are eight things to look for when checking a turtle's health. Except in a young turtle, the shell should be solid. There should be no parasites in the deep folds of the arms and legs. The skin should not have wounds, sores, or white or red spots. The eyes should be open and clear, without swollen lids. The nose and mouth should not have bubbles or foam. The turtle should breathe quietly. Both land and water turtles should walk with the bottom of the shell parallel to the ground, not dragging on one side or in back. The turtle should swim straight, with its back end just a little, but not much, lower than the rest of the body.

Shown below is the plastron, or bottom shell, of a spiny-wheel turtle.

Turtle-tank neutralizer prevents soft shells by adding calcium to a turtle's water. "Happy Turtle" is a sulfa block that helps prevent disease. Both can be found in pet stores.

Like other pets, turtles can have a variety of illnesses or problems. They include fungus, eye infections that cause the eyes to stay closed or to puff up, and small cuts that get infected. A prolapsed intestine will stick out and drag on the ground. A turtle can have constipation, pneumonia, or skin disorders. It also may have parasites, such as amoebas, tapeworm, pinworms, mites, and ticks. It is important to check the turtle regularly for parasites.

If the nose or mouth are bubbly or foamy, or the turtle breathes noisily, it probably has pneumonia. A turtle also may have serious intestinal disorders caused by salmonella. This bacteria is always in the turtle's digestive tract, but it causes problems only occasionally.

Any time a turtle won't eat or is less active, except just before and during hibernation, it probably is ill. The veterinarian can help you treat the turtle with medicine or common household products. If you have more than one turtle, you should have a separate, simple terrarium for the sick turtle.

25

Breeding

All turtles lay their eggs out of the water. Most turtles are three to 12 years old before they are able to become parents. It depends on the species and size of the turtle. The terrarium must be large enough for the male and female turtle to be in the mood to mate. They also are more likely to mate if they are given fresh, tasty food. If they have been ill or do not like the other turtle, they probably will not mate.

If turtles mate, the female will bury about eight eggs. For a water turtle, you must put a dish filled with sand out of the water. The dish must be where the turtle can easily climb up on it. If the turtle lays the eggs in the water, you can rescue them and try to hatch them. Mother turtles have nothing to do with the eggs—or the babies—once the eggs are laid. However, if the eggs have cracks, are oozing a liquid that turns hard, or smell bad, throw them away.

The yellow-headed wood turtle is from South America.

This painted turtle is four months old, but it still has a lot of growing to do.

When the eggs are laid on land, uncover them. To make sure they stay right-side-up, mark the top side with a pencil. Do not use a pen or marker. Fill a very clear plastic box one-third full with damp peat moss. The peat moss should not be soggy. Bury the eggs about two-thirds of the way into the moss and cover the box. Leave a little crack for air to get into the box. The humidity should be around 80–100 percent. The temperature needs to be about 82 degrees F. You can put the container over warm water, using an aquarium heater to maintain the temperature. You can also simply put it in a warm room, keeping an eye on the temperature.

Every four or five days, uncover the box for a short time. Make sure that the water that forms on the inside of the cover doesn't drip on the eggs. If it does, the humidity is too high.

If everything turns out well, baby turtles will hatch out in three to six months.

The Young

The baby turtle breaks the shell of its egg with a small horny point on the top of its jaw. This is the **egg tooth**. In a few hours, the hatchling is out of the shell. The egg tooth soon falls off. The turtle has a two-inch body and a two-inch tail if the adult turtles are the size of a dinner plate. Smaller adults have smaller babies.

A **yolk** sac is attached to the turtle's underside. It provides food for about a week. By then, the turtle will be old enough to eat on its own. The youngsters should have their own terrarium, separate from the adult turtles.

Offer the baby turtles fresh food every day. When they are older, they will begin to eat less often. The food must be chopped to fit the size of the young turtle's mouths. Like adults, they also will need vitamins and minerals. Calcium is especially important for the proper growth of the shell.

Young turtles—even ones this small—should have their own terrariums.

Travel

A turtle can travel for up to six hours in a covered plastic terrarium of about eight gallons. There should be no water in it, even if you're moving a water turtle. Keeping the turtle warm enough is very important. Temperatures below 65 degrees F. make it easy for the turtle to catch a cold or pneumonia. In cool weather, the travel terrarium must have a tight cover. Air slits should be taped shut.

Before leaving home, the travel terrarium should be put into a box that has been lined with layers of newspapers to help keep out the cold. Line the bottom of the terrarium with dry foam rubber so the turtle's claws can get a good grip. Upon arrival, remove the lid in a warm room and fan fresh air into the terrarium.

It is best to board your turtle if you must be gone for a long time. A pet store or your veterinarian may be able to keep the turtle for you.

It's best to avoid taking your turtle on long trips. For shorter trips in warm weather, a travel box like this one works well.

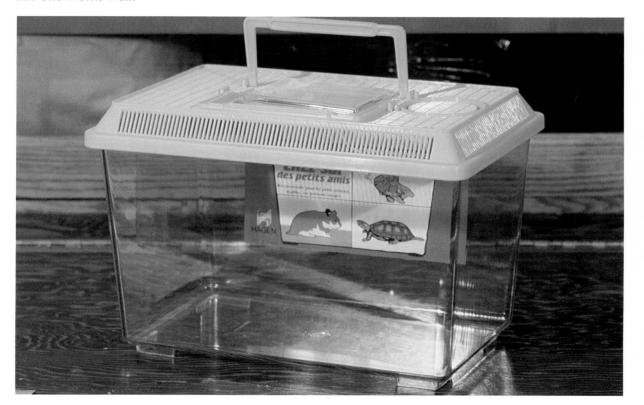

GLOSSARY

Barbels	Pieces of flesh that some turtles have on their heads. Barbels look like worms and attract animals that the turtle then eats.
Carapace	The shell that covers the turtle's back.
Cold-blooded animal	An animal whose temperature changes with the temperature of its surroundings.
Egg tooth	A horny tip on the upper part of a hatching turtle's jaw that helps the baby break out of the eggshell.
Endangered species	A species that has very few members left in its natural area. The animals should not be taken from their area.
Feces	Waste material from the intestines.
Hibernate	To go into a period of inactivity because cold weather slows the body's activities.
Incubate	To warm an egg so the young inside will develop and hatch.
Lamina	The hard material, like fingernails, that covers the turtle's underside.
Plastron	The shell that covers the turtle's underside.
Species	A group of animals that have common characteristics.
Yolk	Food inside an egg used by the developing baby.

INDEX

Photographs by Mark E. Ahlstrom

*We would like to thank the following people
and businesses for their help in making this book:*

The Fish Bowl
Gayle Harrtranft
Bethann "BA" Lord
Jimmy Schmidt
Tropic Waters
Twin Cities Reptiles

Produced by Mark E. Ahlstrom
(The Bookworks)
St. Peter, MN

Typesetting and Keylining: The Final Word
Photo Research: Judith A. Ahlstrom

ONE
WEEK
IN
JANUARY

ONE WEEK IN JANUARY

New Paintings for an Old Diary

By Carson Ellis

CHRONICLE BOOKS

SAN FRANCISCO

"Grace Cathedral Hill"
Words and music by Colin Meloy.
Copyright © 2002 Music of Stage Three (BMI) / Osterozhna! Music (BMI).
All rights administered by BMG Rights Management (US) LLC.
Used by permission. All rights reserved.
BMG controls 100 percent o/b/o Colin Meloy / Osterozhna! Music.

Library of Congress Cataloging-in-Publication Data
Names: Ellis, Carson, 1975- author, illustrator.
Title: One week in January : new paintings for an old diary / by Carson Ellis.
Description: San Francisco : Chronicle Books, [2024]
Identifiers: LCCN 2023059010 | ISBN 9781797216959 (hardcover)
Subjects: LCSH: Ellis, Carson, 1975---Diaries. | Artists--Oregon--
   Portland--Diaries.
Classification: LCC NC975.5.E45 A2 2024 | DDC 741.973--dc23/eng/20240220
LC record available at https://lccn.loc.gov/2023059010

Manufactured in China.

Design by Kristen Hewitt.

10 9 8 7 6 5 4 3 2 1

Chronicle books and gifts are available at special quantity discounts to corporations, professional associations, literacy programs, and other organizations. For details and discount information, please contact our premiums department at corporatesales@chroniclebooks.com or at 1-800-759-0190.

Chronicle Books LLC
680 Second Street
San Francisco, California 94107
www.chroniclebooks.com

INTRODUCTION

A FEW YEARS AGO, I was going through a crate of letters and keep-sakes and found eight typed pages documenting a single week in 2001. I don't usually keep journals, and I didn't remember writing this one. I read it aloud to my husband, Colin, and we laughed. It chronicled the week I moved to Portland, Oregon, and I had recorded only the minu-tiae of each day: what I ate (mostly bagels), what I drank (so much booze), what I listened to (Napster), whether anyone had emailed me (generally not). It was a droning catalog of my life at twenty-five, broke and unemployed, on the cusp of the digital age. I liked it.

I wrote to my old friend Emmy, who appears in it often, and told her I wanted to illustrate this weird, boring journal. I wrote, "I can't remember the thinking behind it."

Emmy did remember. She told me I had begun to fret about forget-ting things—at the age of twenty-five—and that this obsessive record had been a brain exercise to stave off memory loss. Did I read about this strategy somewhere? Did I make it up? I don't, of course, remember. My memory has only gotten worse. The week I moved to Portland would be sinking slowly into oblivion if not for this meticulous journal that brought it all back.

The "new house" I refer to in the journal was not, in fact, a house. It was a 350-square-foot space inside a Southeast Portland warehouse. There was a shared bathroom down the hall, and I used the kitchen (also the phone, the computer, the TV, and the VCR) in the space downstairs where Colin lived with our friend Stiv. There was an additional, inexplicable toilet in Colin and Stiv's kitchen, right next to the fridge, that we called "Plan B."

The three of us were friends from college, and a fourth college friend, Nathan, lived upstairs. Colin worked in a pizza place, and his boss, Zefrey, also a painter, lived in the space next door to mine. Over the next year, I'd get to know just about everyone in the building. My old friend and longtime gallerist, May, would move in next door to Colin and Stiv and run a bookshop and venue out of her tiny space called the Lazy Lady Lounge. This warehouse was home to Portland label Marriage Records; to the bimonthly arts journal, the *Organ*;

to Pinko's, a place where underresourced and unhoused people could access free computers; and to at least three art collectives: the Charm Bracelet, the Alphabet Dress, and Red76. There was always a band practicing in the basement. It was a great scene.

The building was scrappy but cheap and fabulous compared to the unheated San Francisco warehouse I had moved from. I came to Portland with a little money I had earned selling paintings and working as a cocktail waitress in the Bay Area. I made my unemployment stretch as long as I possibly could—surviving on pizza that Colin brought home from work and mooching off my friends—until I finally gave up and went back to work in a bar.

In January 2001, Colin and I were bickering but inseparable friends on the verge of hooking up for the first time. I was still apparently planning trips to Mexico with my ex-boyfriend Matt. My San Francisco boyfriend, Eric, is the guy on the motorbike in the Decemberists song "Grace Cathedral Hill" (called the "New Year's Day song" in this journal). I am the crying person. The green-eyed girl that Colin sings about being sweet on is not me, but my beautiful, good-time San Francisco friend Katie.

Margery, Colin's former long-term girlfriend, plays a big part in this book. Emmy, one of my best friends from high school, went on a few dates with Colin at the time of the journal and would eventually marry Nathan. January 2001 was an era of many entanglements. Now, more than two decades later, it's hard to imagine so many important relationships being so messy. I think it was often painful.

In 2001, I had art shows in people's houses, made comics for zines, and painted with oils on big canvases. I was beginning to field my first illustration inquiries. It was the year the Decemberists played their first shows (in fact, we think the Medicine Hat show mentioned in this journal may have been their *very* first) and recorded their first album, a self-released EP called *5 Songs*. We burned the CDs at home, stamped them with the band's name, and put them in letter-pressed sleeves with our home address printed on them. I drew flyers for shows with Sharpie and copied them at Kinko's. In 2001, Colin and I were working on an illustrated book about a Russian girl named Ruthie Baumbaum, referred to here as "the story." We never finished it, but a decade later we would cannibalize all the good parts to write and illustrate the Wildwood Chronicles. In 2001, nearly everyone

I knew was an artist, a musician, a dancer, or a writer. With a few exceptions, we were all pretty broke.

I'm not especially proud of the impression I make in this journal. I cringe at my twee turns of phrase and my casual mentions of Hemingway and Soviet art films. But I've made a point not to edit it much. I love this twenty-five-year-old me, and I'm not mad at her for trying too hard. I'm a carefully stoic diarist, but beneath all the flatness and comic tedium runs a true current of sorrow and longing. This is the diary of a young artist with no money and few prospects. She's just moved into yet another shabby warehouse, and she's in love with her best friend, who appears to be in love with everyone but her. From the outside, things look dismal, but her life is brimming with possibility. Sometimes she even knows it.

Saturday

SATURDAY, JANUARY 6TH, 2001. I woke up at Colin and Stiv's around nine. Colin asked me to put on the folk anthology and I did. I set up a new email account on Yahoo. I called Matt and he said he'd call me back in a couple of hours, but he never did. Stiv asked me to turn off the folk anthology and I did. I had cereal and bananas for breakfast and then came up here to work on my new house. I plugged in my phone and discovered it works but it's the number of the people who were here before me—Four Wall Cinema—and every time it rang, and I answered it, confusion ensued. I went to the paint store and bought a new sponge for the roller and then painted the wall above my window white. I also repainted the counter red because it was ruined by paint thinner and black spray paint. I unpacked and sorted and organized for a while. Colin came up and asked if he could sing me some new songs. We went downstairs and he played me the song he wrote for the score to *Happiness* that Loser sings to his dead wife, which was really tragic and pretty. He also sang me a song he wrote about New Year's Day when we were walking around San Francisco. This song made me cry because I was in it, and it was about my last day in San Francisco, so I asked Colin to play it again, and he did.

Then we went to lunch at Dots Cafe, which had no windows, so your eyes had to adjust to the dark. I had a Reuben and Colin had a BLT and we split an order of spicy fries. We came home and the buzzer buzzed at Colin and Stiv's, so I picked up the phone and it was Scotty Crawford, passing through town. He came up and I showed him my new house. He went back down to Colin and Stiv's and I did some more unpacking and sorting and organizing. Colin came up to say he was going to work and to tell me to work on illustrations for the story and to ask me if I wanted him to bring me back pizza. I said, "Yes, with pepperonis." Shortly after, Stiv came upstairs with Emmy and Amy, who'd come to visit me. We looked at some pictures and I put on a pair of pants that would prove to be too tight and we went, in Amy's truck, to the Laurelthirst to see James Low's band for happy hour. Margery met us there and also Erin. We stayed for a couple of hours and drank some beer and then Margery and I came back here to my new house after buying a six-pack of Heineken at the Plaid Pantry. Nathan came to visit, and Pete Novak was here too, en route to Missoula, with a new tattoo. He toppled me over onto the futon, spilling beer everywhere. Then everybody left and I struggled to put

together my futon frame. I went back down to Colin and Stiv's and checked my email. Colin came home and said he was going out with Emmy. I had a sweet letter from Eric and a funny letter about monkey sailors from Matt. I wrote them both back and came back up here to finish the futon. Nathan and Pete came back just in time to help me put the whole thing together and then they went upstairs to Nathan's to smoke pot. I started sorting through old pictures and then my across-the-hall neighbor, Sean, came by with milk and cookies. Colin came home and we all looked at pictures and then Colin and I walked to the Plaid Pantry for more Heineken. When we got back, we sat on the futon and drank beer and looked at pictures and listened to the folk anthology for a while. Then Colin went home, and I had one more cigarette on the futon and crawled up into my bed to sleep for the first time in my new house.

Sunday

SUNDAY, JANUARY 7TH, 2001. I woke up and wrote down the day before. I peeked my head in to say good morning to Stiv and then took a shower downstairs. I came back up and sorted my hundreds of photographs by year. Stiv came up and bummed a cigarette before leaving for work. Emmy called and we decided to go for a walk. I went down to Colin and Stiv's, where no one was home, and had a bowl of cereal. Then Emmy came over and we went to Forest Park with her dog, Addie, in my car because hers was leaking coolant. When we got back from our walk it was dark already. We talked about maybe going to Eastern Europe together. I went to Sheridan; bought light bulbs, fake butter, cream cheese, orange juice, an avocado, and a bagel. I made myself dinner at Colin and Stiv's with the ingredients, where still no one was home. I got another funny email from Matt and wrote him back to tell him I had money saved up to go to Mexico. I also got a message from Christian Bruno whose short film got accepted at Sundance. He was calling to ask me to do some sketches for a postcard and possibly some posters for the movie. After dinner, I came back up here and called Matt, who was tired and not fun to talk to. Then I called Margery to say that maybe I'd go out with her and Heidi, but it would be later because I was in a quiet mood at the moment. I went back to sorting pictures: took my favorite pictures from each year and put them in a big pile, in perfect chronological order, starting on March 1993 and ending on December 2000. Then I found spaces for all my things, swept and mopped the floor, attempted to assemble my drawing table but discovered, to my dismay, it was missing a crucial piece. I stole a shower rack from the bathroom on which I put all my clothes. I put light bulbs in all my lights and got Colin's down comforter from his room to put on my futon. Margery called to see if I'd go out, but I didn't feel like it. Colin came over with pizza and then left to make flyers at Kinko's. I finished Stiv's novel. I read pages 185–256 and didn't finish until one a.m. I went downstairs and Colin and Stiv were watching the very end of *Naked*. I watched with them and then borrowed *Under Milk Wood* by Dylan Thomas from Colin. I read the first 25 pages aloud and went to sleep.

Monday

MONDAY, JANUARY 8TH, 2001. Colin came and knocked on my door, waking me up, to tell me he was getting bagels. I was really tired but went downstairs to have breakfast. I checked my email, and no one had written me. Stiv called his haircutter friend to make an appointment for me, but the salon was closed on Mondays. Colin went out to hang flyers and I came back up here and wrote down the day before. Afterwards, I went downstairs and talked to Stiv about his book. I checked my email and still no one had written me, but I wrote an email to Christian and his friend Cat about making postcards for the movie. Colin came home and I told him and Stiv that I was taking the ugly painting above the door to paint over. Stiv said it was his painting so whatever I painted over it would be his too, but I disagreed. Colin and Stiv talked about whether they liked the movie *Naked* and then Colin said he was really late for work and left. Stiv went to buy a new CD player and I came back up here. I started a painting of people flying on the long stretcher and I covered the ugly painting with a quart of green latex to get rid of the raised circles underneath, but it didn't really work. I made three sketches for the movie, and I read *Under Milk Wood* one and a half times aloud. I went

downstairs to bug Stiv. He was talking on the phone and listening to his new stereo. I checked my email again but still no one had written me. I wrote another email to Cat asking whether or not there should be text on the postcard. Stiv played a bunch of different stuff on the stereo and showed me how loud it was. I went to Colin's bookshelf and remembered he had told me to read a book by Ernest Hemingway, but I couldn't remember which one. I figured out it was *The Sun Also Rises*, but Stiv said that I should read *Narcissus and Goldmund* instead. I said, "Okay," and took the book plus Colin's book on socialist realist painting, an ashtray, and a Coke up to my room. I hadn't been here very long when Stiv told me Eric was on the phone. I ran downstairs and ran back up here with the phone. He told me there was a live web-cam at my old house and he would go make faces into the camera for me while we talked on the phone. I persuaded him to come for a visit and we made a date to talk on the phone again on Thursday once my phone is hooked up. Colin had come in during the conversation and showed me he had bought the Corn Sisters CD. I went downstairs but, when I walked in, Colin scowled at me because he was playing music and I had interrupted him. He was playing the song about New Year's

Day, and I said if he would play it once I would let him practice. He did, so I did and came back up here and read a little but mostly just stared into space. Colin came up and we went to Sheridan to get wine, but it was closed so we came back here, grabbed my movies, and drove to Zupan's, where we bought a bottle of Concha y Toro. I had no money or wallet on me, and Colin was annoyed because I never have money and said I had to buy the next two bottles of wine. Next, we went to the video store to drop off the movies, but I made Colin go in to return them because I didn't want to see the crazy girl that works there, and I couldn't remember if I'd even paid for them to begin with. When we got home, Stiv and Zefrey were playing chess and Colin began working on a song, so I decided to check my email again but still no one had written me. I went to the Seemen website to see the live webcam at my old house, but it wasn't working. Colin and I came back up here, and he read some of this journal. Then Stiv and Zefrey came up and Colin read more of it, and everybody laughed because it was so boring. Then a fight broke out between an old guy at Sheridan and a crazy guy who had been dumpster diving. They were yelling at each other, and we all climbed up on the counter and yelled, "FIGHT!

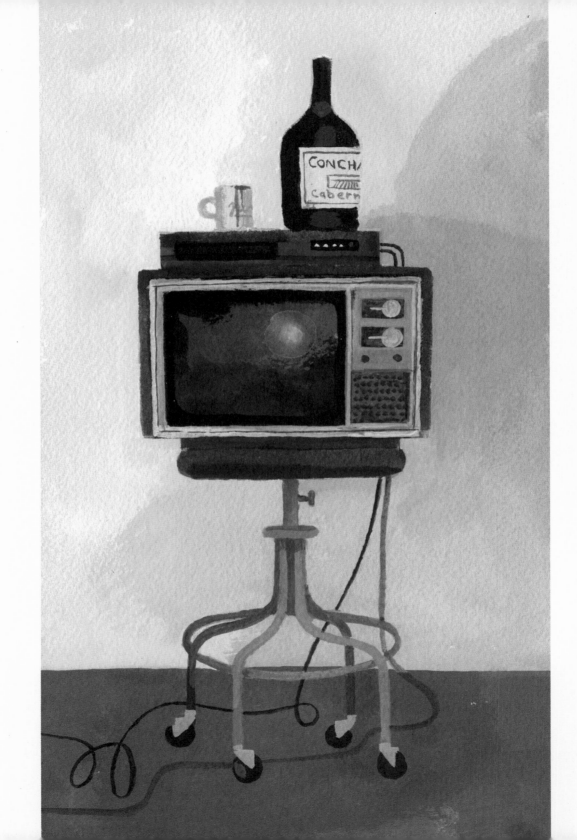

FIGHT! FIGHT!" out the windows. Stiv and Zefrey went next door to play chess at Zefrey's and Colin and I went downstairs to watch movies. First, we watched *I Break for Cycles*, then *Happiness*, which Colin is writing a score for. He played along and I would stop it and rewind and tape-record the stuff that sounded good. Stiv came home midway through the movie and said he'd lost three games in a row and went to sleep. Colin watched almost to the end and went to sleep too. I watched the whole thing and came back up here and worked on the long canvas, then went to Texaco and bought two packs of cigarettes and Pork Cup O' Noodles. I went to Colin and Stiv's and put water on for the Cup O' Noodles and checked my email one more time but still no one had written me. I made the soup and left a pack of Camels on Stiv's desk because I had smoked his last one. On my way back up, I ran into Nathan, and he came over and we chatted for a while. We talked about his best friend being mad at him, *Under Milk Wood*, Stiv's book, and how we haven't been good artists lately. Then Nathan went to sleep, and I got into bed and read the first chapter of *Narcissus and Goldmund* and went to sleep myself.

Tuesday

CENTER STAIR
ROOF ACCESS

2

B1 THROUGH 5

EX

FIRE EXI

NO
KEEP D
CLOSED
ALL T

TUESDAY, JANUARY 9TH, 2001. I woke up and went straight down to Colin and Stiv's for breakfast. Stiv was on the computer and Colin was out buying bagels. I decided to have cereal instead though, and to save my bagel for lunch. Over breakfast we talked about how gross and frequent my smoking habit is. I decided to try to smoke less, but then I went upstairs and smoked two cigarettes while I wrote down the day before. I then got all my shower stuff together and went to ask Stiv to call his hairdresser friend. He gave me the number and I made an appointment for the next day at one p.m. He told me there was a message for me on the machine that turned out to be someone named Sam Green who was the guy that Christian had made his movie with. He was calling to leave his number in case I had to get in touch with him for any reason. I took a shower and came back upstairs and fucked around, walking around in my underwear, and doing nothing for a while before I decided to run some errands. I got dressed and went downstairs to find my shoes, which turned up under Colin and Stiv's couch. I asked Stiv where the photo store was and where I could buy a smoke detector. He told me and asked if I could mail something at the post office for him and I said I could. First, I walked to the photo store to buy Mylar tape and nylon gloves, but they were out of tape, so I ordered some. Next, I went to the post office, but I didn't feel like waiting in line, so I put two dollars' worth of postage on Stiv's manila envelope and stuffed it in a mail slot. Then, on the way home, I looked for the hardware store on Ankeny for the smoke detector but never found it. When I got back, I went to Colin and Stiv's where no one was home and toasted my bagel for lunch with fake butter, cream cheese, avocado, and pepper. I checked my email and there was a nice long letter from Vanessa. I listened to my favorite Napster songs, smoked a cigarette, and wrote her back. Then I came upstairs and worked on the long canvas for a while. When I got bored of it, I started another painting of flying people on a squarish canvas that featured all the characters from the book that Colin and I are writing: Ruthie, Mr. Baumbaum, the orphanage undesirables, the handsome factory worker, the monkey, Misha the maid, the mysterious soldier, the French chef, the talking donkey, a pirate, the mute hag, a thief, the stripped tank part salesman, and a cat. I went back downstairs and checked my email again. This time I had a letter from Brian and Cherri inviting me to create a proposal to decorate a shark for a

San Jose public art thing. The honorarium was a thousand dollars, and I wrote them back to say I was interested and to tell them my idea. I then called Colin to ask him to bring me pepperoni pizza home for dinner and he said he would. I came back and worked on the squarish canvas a bit and then fell asleep on the futon. When I woke up, Colin had come in with pizza. I gobbled it up and Colin left for band practice. I went downstairs and played on the computer some but then Colin came in with his band because they'd decided to practice there, so I left. I came back to my house and read *Narcissus and Goldmund* for an hour or so but decided I didn't like it. There was a loud scary rap at the door, and it was Stiv and Margery, on their way to a party. I put on my coat, and we grabbed Colin and left. When we got to the party, it was less than ten really high strangers sitting around in a living room, so we all felt weird and left quickly. We then went to a bar called Caswell's where Margery and I drank wine, and the boys drank Guinness. We played MASH—normal for Colin and then evil MASH, where everyone else gets to choose terrible things for you. Halfway through Stiv's turn, a fight broke out at the bar. Some glass got broken and there was a lot of yelling. The bartender closed out our tab because she'd decided she'd had enough and was up and leaving so we went to the bar next door called My Father's Place. Here we drank dollar PBRs and stayed until two-thirty or so, talking about health care and making fun of the tough guys from Caswell's. Colin left after a beer but the rest of us got a second and had to chug it when the bartender came by and told us to leave. Margery went home and Stiv and I walked back here. I got home and read for a little and went to sleep.

Wednesday

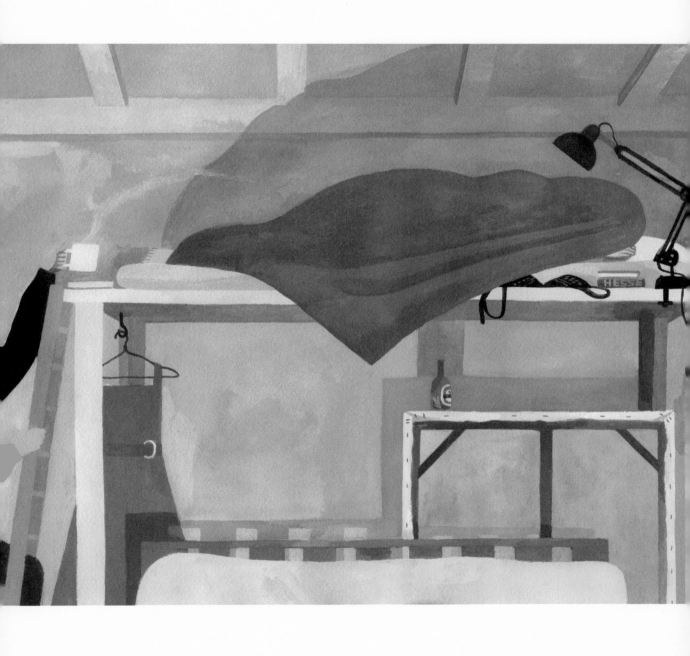

WEDNESDAY, JANUARY 10ᵀᴴ, 2001. I woke up to the building man-ager knocking on the door. She told me the owners of the building wouldn't pay to have a phone line installed for my house, which costs eighty-five dollars, because they consider the phone to be a luxury. I crawled back into bed and soon Colin came up to tell me to get ready for breakfast because it was 11:15 and Margery was coming at 11:30 to go with us. I got up and got dressed and we went downstairs. Stiv told us that Margery had called to say she actually wasn't coming so we left for the Stepping Stone. Colin had scrambled eggs and sausage and I had eggs over medium and we played five and pass it. Then we went downtown for my haircut from Stiv's friend, Rachel. Colin got his hair cut after me. We almost finished the crossword while Rachel cut our hair and then we each paid her thirty dollars and also bought a tin of hair wax for fourteen dollars, which we shared. I liked my hair-cut pretty well and thought Colin's looked good too, but he hated it. We then came home briefly to get some stuff and went to our respec-tive banks. I deposited the seventy-five-dollar check from my uncle for Hanukkah. Then we went to the post office to pick up a package that was waiting there for me. I was excited, but it turned out to be a caller ID from the phone company, which was disappointing. We came home and Colin left for work, and I took a shower. I came upstairs and looked at myself in the mirror for a while, admiring my new haircut. I went downstairs and checked my email. Christian had written to remind me to call his friend Sam Green and Cat had written to tell me not to include text and to email the images instead of faxing them, which I, of course, don't know how to do. Nathan came in and we talked about the San Jose shark thing and the prospect of buying a big warehouse like this one. I heated us up some pizza from yesterday. Then I came up here and made four sketches for *Pie Fight '69*. I went back downstairs and checked the messages. Michael Hecht had called saying he was putting a check in the mail for me. Emmy and my mom had both called, asking me to call them back. I called Emmy and asked her to come to my housewarming party on Friday, but she didn't want to because she didn't know or like anyone coming. Colin came home midway through the conversation and he and Emmy managed to have an argument through me, relaying things from one to the other. I got off the phone and Colin and I decided to go to the Rabbit Hole and get a glass of wine. At the Rabbit Hole we each had a glass of red

wine and a bowl of soup. I had clam chowder and Colin had French onion. We talked about how much Valentine's Day would suck, then I remembered I was going to *La Bohème* with Margery. Colin moped and said he thought he would get to go instead of me, and I said if he was going to mope about it maybe he could just have my ticket. Then we came home to work on the story. We were too lazy to get wine, so we drank Kahlúa and vanilla soy milk. We wrote Katie Parsons an email; Colin wrote her a sappy poem because he's in love with her. We then worked on the story for a while. I did a bunch of sketches and Colin wrote. At twelve-thirty Colin went to sleep, and I came back up here and looked at an art magazine of Stiv's and did nothing and went to bed around two-thirty.

Thursday

THURSDAY, JANUARY 11TH, 2001. I woke up to Stiv and the phone company guy, who had let themselves in. The phone company guy put a contraption into the phone jack and Stiv said that the phone company guy would need to get back in, so I had to get up, but I went back to sleep instead. Soon Colin came in and crawled into bed with me and I told him about my scary dream from the night before: I woke up in my bed after having a nightmare and when I closed my eyes to go back to sleep, the bed started moving up and down. I opened my eyes, but once I closed them again to sleep the bed moved again. It happened a couple more times until I fell back asleep in my dream. Colin left and I went downstairs to take a shower. I came back up and wrote down the day before. The phone company guy had disappeared, never to return. I went downstairs and Colin said there was a note on the front door of the building from the phone company guy saying he had come by but couldn't get in. This was strange as he'd already been in the building and was instructed to ring Colin and Stiv's to get back in. I called the phone company, and the operator told me that, since the computer was telling her that the order was still open, the phone company guy was probably still in the vicinity. We decided to go downtown. I grabbed the note from the phone company guy off the door and found it was weird and illegible. We looked for him on surrounding telephone poles, but he had vanished, so we walked downtown and had Thai food for lunch. I had pad thai and Colin had panang with tofu. After, we walked around aimlessly for a while. We went to a bookstore, a glasses store, and saw a natural amphitheater in a square. Colin said I should make an illustrated version of *Under Milk Wood*, and I said, "That's a good idea." We went to Nordstrom's so I could put on some lipstick and then saw a matinee: *Quills*, about the Marquis de Sade, which was awful. We heckled through the whole thing and debated leaving but ultimately sat through it and then walked home. When we got back Stiv was sitting at his desk with some candles lit, reading. "Where were you guys?" he asked.

"We saw the horrible movie about the Marquis de Sade," I said.

"No, you didn't," said Stiv.

"Yes, we did," said I. We discovered that Stiv had gone to meet us at the movies and had seen the same bad movie at the same place and

time but in the theater next door. (It was playing on two screens simultaneously.) We talked about how bad it was and then Stiv went to Sheridan and bought three bottles of wine. We convinced him to open one and then we drank it. Nathan came down and we sat around chatting until Stiv and Colin got into a nasty fight about something stupid. Colin left for the Medicine Hat where he was playing a show. Stiv said he needed to have a heart-to-heart with Colin, and we agreed. Then Nathan and I went to Burger King for dinner and then to Kinko's to scan and email my *Pie Fight* sketches. Afterwards, we drove to the Medicine Hat to see the Decemberists. Two guys from Missoula played some cowboy songs first. Margery was there, as well as Colin's friend December, who promotes bands. Stiv, Mazanna, and her girlfriend showed up a little later. Chantelle was there too, and Colin talked to both her and December about the possibility of my doing some band posters for them. Colin played a really nice set, including the New Year's Day song. Nathan and Stiv took my car home, and I went home later with Colin. We listened to Iris DeMent in the car and then I slept over at Colin's.

Friday

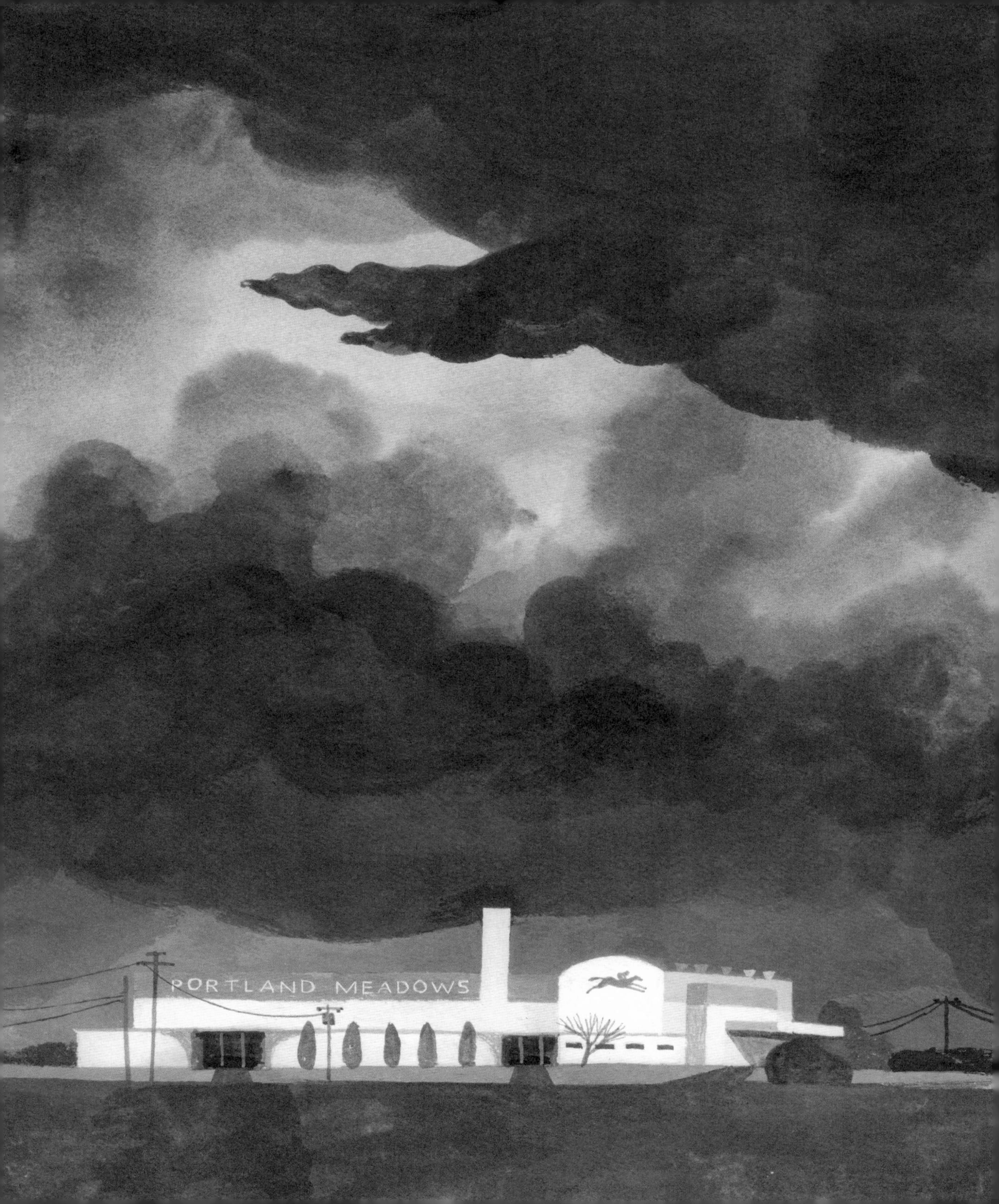
PORTLAND MEADOWS

FRIDAY, JANUARY 12TH, 2001. Colin and I woke up and made a bet on how many minutes long the music was that he had composed to *Happiness*. Colin said five minutes and I said fifteen and the answer was nine, so I lost by a minute or so and had to go to Sheridan and buy breakfast. We had bagels and coffee, and I checked my email to discover that the sketches I'd sent Cat had come right back to me. Colin tried to figure out how to shrink them down (they were enormous) and send them back to Cat. I went upstairs and wrote down my day and then came back downstairs to shower. After my shower, I went to Colin and Stiv's to call the phone company and yell at people. December was over and she and Colin went to lunch. The phone company said they'd send someone as soon as they could. I started working on a flyer for the Decemberists. First, I drew the funeral procession for the mechanical boy prince of Persia. Then I checked my email and had a letter from Jen. I wrote her back and then there was a tremendously loud knock on the door. It was a kid from the phone company. He said, "I have some bad news . . ." He tried to explain some things to me that I didn't understand about outside vendors and then we went upstairs to look at my phone jack, which still had the contraption from the weird, old phone guy from the day before in it. I was so angry at the phone company that I was mean to the kid out of frustration and felt immediately sorry for it. He said he would go check out some stuff outside and then come find me at Colin and Stiv's when he was done. I went back to the computer and wrote Eric a letter about the phone company. Then Colin and December came back from lunch, and I began to look for pictures of Victorian era wrestlers on the Internet for the second flyer idea. I never found any, but I did find a website made by a guy named Mr. Self-Destruct that featured airbrushed portraits of professional wrestlers and wrestling posable dolls in wrestling positions, pictures of friends, family, and Chihuahuas, all accompanied by funny industrial/video game sounding music. December, Colin, and I went upstairs to look at my posters. I didn't have anything to say about them and Colin later told me that I have to sell myself more. December left, Colin played on the computer, and I worked on the mechanical boy prince flyer. Colin called Emmy and asked her if she wanted to come to the track with us. She did so we picked her up and went to Portland Meadows to bet on horses. It was rainy and we drove down MLK instead of I-5 and got sort of lost. Colin was being a real brat. To everything that Emmy and I asked, he would say, "No," and when I patted him on the shoulder he said, "Don't touch me."

I said, "You're never coming to the track with me again, are you?"

He said, "No."

I said, "That's mean."

He said, "Good," and I said in my head, "I hate Colin Meloy."

We got to the track in time for the third race and I told Colin that I was so mad and went to buy a program, a hotdog, and a beer. I placed my first bet—two dollars across on the number six—and went to the paddock to look at my horse. Then I saw Colin and was still angry, so he half-heartedly apologized, and we made up. The only good bet either of us made was the same bet: three bucks across on a long

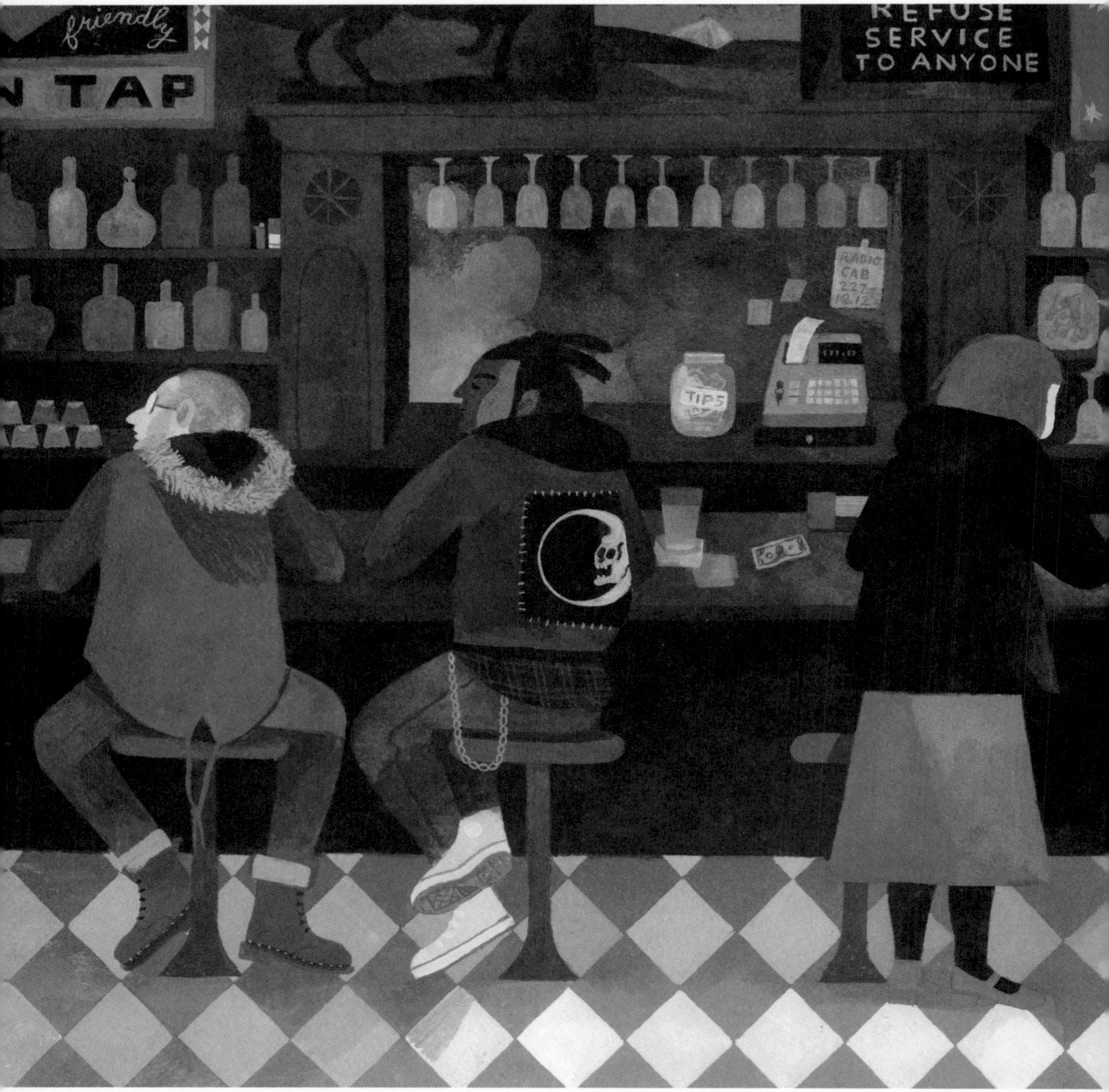
friendly
N TAP
REFUSE
SERVICE
TO ANYONE
RADIO
CAB
TIPS

shot and we both won twenty-four dollars. Emmy made one bet on a

horse named the Cisco Kido in the fifth race and lost. I was wearing

Emmy's grandma's rings, my red dress, and red high heels for luck.

Our luck was never very good though, and we left after the sixth race.

We dropped Emmy at home and came back to the warehouse where

I fell asleep on Colin and Stiv's couch for about an hour. Nathan

woke me up at ten of ten and the three of us walked downtown to see

Margery, Lucia, and Heidi in a dance performance at an art school. I

kept slipping and falling all the way there because of my lucky shoes.

When we got there, it had just ended, and we all felt dumb for miss-

ing it. I walked around and looked at the art, which was bad except

for a painting of a rooster on a pane of glass. Heidi then drove Colin,

Nathan, and me to a bar called XV where we got so drunk. Colin

drank screwdrivers, Nathan drank beer, and I drank Scotch. I started

talking to a boy named Donald and Colin pretended to be my jeal-

ous boyfriend. Then I slipped and fell on the ramp going down to the

bathroom because of drunkenness and, again, the lucky red shoes. I

broke two glasses—one with Scotch, the other with water—and two men rushed over to help me up and brush me off. I was sad because my Scotch was now on my dress but one of the men offered to buy me another, so I didn't care. Then Margery came and introduced me to a guy named Seantos, in Elvis sunglasses, who was some sort of promoter or something. We talked about me making some posters for him and exchanged numbers and the owner of the bar bought me another Scotch because I had fallen down and broken mine. I went back to talk to Donald, but he told me he was looking for his one true love and tucked my hair behind my ear, so I left and sat down with Lucia, Jebediah, Colin, Margery, Nathan, and some of Jebediah's friends. Nathan was sad because the hot girl that he hadn't worked up the courage to talk to had left. Colin and I started singing Pogues songs as loud as we could and slamming our fists on the table. The bouncer came by and told us to shut up, but we didn't. Another guy, collecting glasses, said to us snidely, "Is that really necessary?" but still we sang. I vowed never to return. Then we got up to go home and Nathan tried to solicit a ride from Margery, who was in the midst of a conversation, and I said we ought to walk anyway because we were so drunk. A couple of blocks from home, we spotted some scaffolding on the roof of a building with thirty-foot ladders tied to either side. Nathan somehow got onto the fire escape and busted the chain that was securing the lowest part of the ladder and keeping it from touching the ground. (It was one of those seesaw type ladders.) It was raining now, and I ran to get Nathan's bag and slipped and fell on my ass. We climbed the fire escape to the roof and Nathan got out his video camera. Colin and I each climbed a ladder on either side of the scaffolding. I was still wearing high heels and climbed so carefully. When we got to the top, we were dozens of feet up with about thirty feet between us. After some time, Colin put a cigarette in his mouth and yelled to me, "Do you have a light?"

I yelled back, "Yes. Come down and we'll have a cigarette."

So, we climbed down and ran around on the roof, going up some more ladders and looking into a creepy brick room. Nathan had filmed the whole thing, so we went home to watch it. When we got back on the ground, we started running and I yelled, "Wait you guys!" and fell on

my ass once more. I had left my red candle that I stole from the bar on the ground next to the building, but I couldn't find it and decided to come back for it the next day. We walked home in the rain and went straight up to Nathan's. First, we watched the rap video that we made in San Francisco for "Va Va Vonya" which was so funny. Then we watched the video of the roof, which was beautiful and eerie with only the noise of cars on the highway and some yelling in the background. We shared the last two cigarettes and the last two beers between the three of us. Nathan rewound the tape, and we watched the whole thing again with outtakes from "Va Va Vonya," scenes of Colin and Nathan driving out to San Francisco, and some video shot at the Shanghai. Colin went to sleep, and Nathan and I talked about lost love.

"Now I'm sad," I said.

"Now I'm really sad," said Nathan. I kissed him goodnight on the cheek and went to bed.